DEACONESS MARGARET RODGERS

A WOMAN IN A MAN'S WORLD

EDITED BY ERIN MOLLENHAUER

The Latimer Trust

The Latimer Trust (formerly Latimer House, Oxford) is a conservative evangelical research organisation within the Church of England, whose main aim is to promote the history and theology of Anglicanism as understood by those in the Reformed tradition. Interested readers are welcome to consult its website for further details of its many activities.

The Latimer Trust

London N14 4PS UK

Registered Charity: 1084337

Company Number: 4104465

Web: www.latimertrust.org

E-mail: administrator@latimertrust.org

Sadly, I did not have the opportunity to meet Margaret Rodgers in person. And yet, this book about her life has given me a profound sense of gratitude for the indelible influence she has had on my own. As I read, I marvelled at the likeness of her and my stories – from the Bachelor of Arts we both studied (at the same institution), to the Bachelor of Divinity we both completed (at different institutions), to the same church we both attended (decades apart), to the research officer role we both filled (her at a national level and I at a diocesan one). But of course, my story is only analogous to hers because she wrote the pages first. I, and so many other women in ministry – both lay and ordained – are, in no small part, able to tread the path we do because Margaret was its pioneer. I'm deeply thankful for this account of a godly woman in a man's world. But I'm even more thankful for this remarkable woman of God, and her life of Christlike service.

The Rev'd Dr Danielle Treweek Deacon and Research Officer in the Anglican Diocese of Sydney.

What shines through in this account of Margaret Rodgers' achievement and influence is the obvious deep love she had for her Lord and Saviour, Jesus Christ. How else can one account for her steady resolve in encouraging women called to serve in ministry and her dedication to the greater Anglican Fellowship? The work God had put before her was not for the faint of heart. In reading this account of her work, I am struck by her evident gifts of diplomacy and her ability to work alongside others with differing theological views for the sake of the gospel. With our current penchant for *cancel culture*, we would do well to learn from her godly example. It is a privilege to continue the work of Anglican Deaconess Ministries that women like Margaret had shaped.

Mary Un is the CEO of Anglican Deaconess Ministries. She believes that women and children, particularly when vulnerable, deserve nothing short of excellence from the organisations serving them. It is a privilege to serve her Lord Jesus by raising up women for him.

This book captures the remarkable life of a woman committed to her Lord and loyal to her church. As her successor, I came to appreciate her drive and energy for media work, despite lacking a media background. While some are formidable to a fault, Margaret was formidable for a purpose.

Russell Powell, CEO of Anglican Media Sydney and Media Adviser to Archbishops Jensen, Davies and Raffel.

I saw Margaret Rodgers from two perspectives – the Newsroom of the Sydney Morning Herald and from the Anglican Media Council: she straddled both worlds admirably. Because she knew the intricacies of Sydney Anglicanism so well, from the first day she ran the media office for the evangelical diocese, she could play a straight bat with the media – she knew what she was talking about, and on the rare occasions she didn't she soon found out. She genuinely cared for the journalists, even the combative ones, and I think they knew that.

After 29 years at the Sydney Morning Herald and the other Fairfax media papers, John Sandeman found it hard to give up the newspaper habit and founded Eternity, a national Christian newspaper for Australia.

Contents Page

Preface

Deaconess Margaret Rodgers AM (1939–2014) was the subject of the Donald Robinson Library Lectures, held at Moore Theological College on 23 September 2023. She was appointed Member of the Order of Australia in January 2014 for service to the Anglican Church of Australia, granting her the post-nominals AM.

The Library Lectures have had a distinguished history, focusing on highly influential figures such as T C Hammond, Samuel Marsden, Deaconess Mary Andrews, D Broughton Knox and H W K Mowll. The most recent lectures have also been published by Latimer Trust.

The term 'deaconess' is well-known among Sydney Anglicans but may be unfamiliar to readers elsewhere, although deaconess orders exist in many other countries. The word was first used in the early church for women with a pastoral ministry, such as Phoebe in Rom 16:1. Deaconess orders grew up as organised movements in mid-nineteenth century Europe in the Lutheran, Methodist and Anglican churches. Many deaconesses were employed by parish churches to perform pastoral duties. Others were also teachers and nurses. Deaconesses do not take vows of celibacy and are free to marry if they wish. They are lay women and thus distinct from women who are ordained to the office of deacon.

Peter Jensen (Chapter 1) introduces this book with an overview of Margaret's life and ministry, and provides unique insight into her character and personality. **Colin Bale** outlines the history of the Deaconess order in Sydney (Chapter 2), and provides an excellent overview of the ministry of Deaconesses. He then analyses Margaret's work as Principal of Deaconess House (Chapter 3). This chapter also includes reminiscences of Margaret from some women who were students during this time. **Kara Hartley** (Chapter 4) discusses her involvement in the Synod of the Diocese of Sydney, including her pioneering work in the establishment of the Doctrine Commission. **Rod Benson** (Chapter 5) investigates her work as Media Officer for the Diocese and CEO of Anglican Media, as well as her extensive involvement in ecumenical activities. We were unfortunately not able to obtain contributions on her involvement with her local parish, the General Synod, Moore Theological College; or her status as a single woman in ministry. The tenth anniversary of her death seems a fitting time to publish the first substantial analysis of her work and legacy.

The choice of Deaconess Margaret Rodgers as the topic of these lectures arose from a desire to honour one of the most significant women, and one of the most significant laypeople, in the history of the Anglican Diocese of Sydney. The scope of her ministry covered an extraordinary range of activities, and she seemed to have a particular talent for committee work. As Rod Benson's chapter shows, she dedicated her annual leave and spare time to committee involvement above and beyond that which was required for her employment with the Diocese. Committee membership may seem uninteresting to some, but it is essential for the good management of any organisation, and Margaret chose to use her intellectual and administrative capabilities to serve the church in this way.

The phrase 'a woman in a man's world' was used by most of the contributors at some point in their papers to summarise Margaret's pioneering role, not only as the first woman member of the Standing Committee, but also as a solo woman in many other male-dominated spaces. It is a curious phrase to use of a member of the Deaconess order, a female-only organisation, but Margaret ventured where no Deaconess had gone before – into Synod, onto other charity boards, and into the fierce world of the media. She earned the respect of everyone she worked with through her many evident gifts and her single-minded devotion to service in administrative roles. Rev Lu Piper recalls, as quoted in Colin Bale's chapter, that Margaret encouraged her to pursue ordination to the diaconate, when this path opened to women in Sydney in 1989. It may seem surprising that Margaret herself never pursued ordination, but this book demonstrates that she was doing the academic, administrative and media work to which she was exceptionally well suited and in which she has left a lasting legacy. Remaining a lay person also allowed her to join a wider range of Synod committees, than she could if she were a deacon.

This dedication to her work and her committee participation appears to be one of the reasons she never married. Her health concerns may have been another reason. Unlike the wives of senior clergy, who often hold honorary roles by virtue of marriage, Margaret's many appointments were achieved through her own efforts and talents. Singleness freed her to devote her life to the service of the church. It is no coincidence that the two women who have been honoured with Library Lectures so far – Margaret Rodgers and Mary Andrews – are single women who spent their lives in undivided devotion to the Lord (1 Cor 7:35).

Moore College Library is the repository for the archives of Anglican Deaconess Ministries and its predecessors including Deaconess House. This collection includes Margaret's academic gown! The Library's full set of *Southern Cross* includes her regular contributions, and her thesis is held in the Reference collection. The records of the Synod are held by the Diocesan Archives. We are not aware of any collection of Margaret's personal papers, but given that her committee involvement stretched far into her personal life, it is possible that she didn't create many documents of her own.

I would like to acknowledge the assistance of Rev Jan Donohoo, in compiling the reminiscences of women who studied under Margaret at Deaconess House, and obtaining their permission to include these in Colin Bale's chapter. Several contributors were ably assisted by the Sydney Diocesan Archivist, Dr Louise Trott, and greatly appreciate this help. The events, kitchen, communications and IT teams at Moore College provided essential support for the Lectures, and ensured an enjoyable and smooth-running event.

Erin Mollenhauer

Senior Archivist and Special Collections Librarian, Moore College

Contributors

The Rev Dr Colin Bale is an Emeritus Faculty member of Moore Theological College. He previously served as Vice-Principal and Head of Church History. He is the author of 'A Crowd of Witnesses: Epitaphs on First World War Australian War Graves' (Longueville, 2015).

Dr Rod Benson is the Donald Robinson Library's Research Support Officer. He was previously Public Affairs Director for the NSW Council of Churches and succeeded Deaconess Margaret Rodgers as a presenter on radio 2CH.

The Ven. Kara Hartley is the Archdeacon for Women's Ministry in the Sydney Anglican Diocese. She is involved with teaching the Bible to women at events, conferences and retreats; meeting with and supporting women in ministry, and recruiting and training women for ministry.

The Rt Rev Dr Peter Jensen was Principal of Moore Theological College from 1985–2001, and the eleventh Archbishop of Sydney from 2001–2013.

1. Margaret Rodgers – An Introduction to her Life

Peter Jensen

Eulogies have their value. They are moments when we express and minister to grief; they recreate the person in a way in which we can be thankful for them; they are like a beautiful portrait in which it is truly the person we are remembering, but with no ill-points on view.

In the case of someone who has played a distinguished public role, there emerges the next stage, some years on, a stage we have reached, when critical history emerges. By critical, I don't mean nasty or opposed. Here, at a distance, we have the opportunity for more considered judgement, for thoughtful description; for context and assessment of contributions made to institutions and movements which are still with us.

That is why I am so glad that we are reflecting on our friend Margaret Rodgers. She is worthy of our memory and the ongoing memory of Sydney Diocese and beyond. She made a lasting contribution to movements, institutions and to persons, both in Australia and in the worldwide Anglican Communion, a contribution recognised by becoming a Member of the Order of Australia in 2014. She helped make us who we are, and it is altogether appropriate that we should begin the task of assessing her person, her times and her achievements.

For our motive is not merely to reflect on a friend. We do well to think of our saints and heroes of earlier times and never forget them. They create our narrative, and their stories enable us to live Christianly in our own day. The life of Margaret is one which must not be forgotten in our time, for it is part of the fabric of our history, and history makes us.

My task is merely to introduce this book. Others will be giving the papers which will make history. Thus, I am going to attempt to give a brief outline, first of Margaret's life, second her ministry, and third her person.

Her Life

As far as an outline of Margaret's life is concerned, I am blessed to have access to a document prepared by Dr Robert Tong submitted in support of her Order of Australia, and also a biographical contribution made by Dr Rod Benson to the *Australian Evangelical Dictionary of Biography.*[1]

Margaret was born in Dorrigo, New South Wales, on 18 December 1939 and died in Sydney on 31 May 2014. That she was granted over seventy years of life was wonderful, in the sense that her health from her teenage years was severely compromised through rheumatic fever. She did well at school and when she entered Deaconess House she achieved her Licenciate in Theology with honours and later graduated from Sydney University with a Bachelor of Arts. In 1977, she was also awarded the Bachelor of Divinity with honours from Sydney University. In my mind, had opportunity allowed, she could have gone on to further study.

Margaret taught History and Divinity at Abbotsleigh and Meriden schools, and became a Deaconess in 1970. From 1969 she began to tutor at Deaconess House, and in 1973 she became the Warden of the Church of England Women's Hall in Glebe. Between 1976 and 1984 she was Principal of Deaconess House and lectured in Church History at Moore Theological College and then moved to the General Synod Office as Administrative and Research Officer, an interesting career shift. In 1994, however, she succeeded Charlotte Rivers as the CEO of Anglican Media and in 2004 was the Archbishop's Media Officer, a post she retired from in 2007.

This is merely the outline. Time does not permit to describe all the committees and boards of which she was a member. Her church was St Stephen's Newtown, of which she was a Church Warden, nominator, reader and a Synod representative. She was a prominent member of the Sydney Synod and the first woman to be elected to its Standing Committee; she was also on the General Synod, its Standing Committee and its Doctrine Commission; she served on the National Council of Churches, the Anglican Consultative Council; she was joint President of the Christian Council of Asia, and a delegate to the World Council of Churches meeting in Canberra. She was a board member of World Vision, chair of the New College Board, and there is more. She wrote, she broadcast over radio 2CH for 13 years, and she was my media officer.

---

1 Rod Benson, "Margaret Amelia Rodgers," in *Australian Dictionary of Biography Online*, ed. Paul F. Cooper (Sydney: Evangelical History Association, 2023) https://sites.google.com/view/australian-dictionary-of-evang/q-r/rodgers-margaret-amelia-1939-2014.

But a list of committees and jobs hardly tells the story. How can we best describe her?

Her ministry

My own guess is that Margaret had her struggles and these helped define her. The first, of course, was with her health. She did not discuss this with me, but I certainly was under the impression that she did not expect to have a long life. She would have been vulnerable on that count and would have developed ways of coping.

Secondly, she was a woman in a man's world. In this she pioneered the path of women in the area of theological education and church politics in a way which was notably different from her distinguished predecessor, Mary Andrews. She took such practical steps as no longer requiring the women students to wear a uniform. She had the academic skills to teach at Moore Theological College, and she worked hard at integrating the women into the experience of Moore while retaining the distinctives of a women's college. In my memory, she became in essence a faculty member of Moore as well as retaining her role at Deaconess House. As a woman, she was on her own in this masculine faculty; but there is no doubt that she held her own. She was preparing the students for a new world of women's ministry and doubtless in her own mind the ordination of women and their leadership role in the churches. All of this involved change, and frequently change that was not welcomed.

Thirdly, she was a Christian in an increasingly unbelieving world. Like us all, she was navigating the waters of secularism and seeking ways to promote the gospel of Jesus and to guard the faith against the assaults of unbelief. Nor was this simply in the world; Margaret was an evangelical Christian from the small outpost of Sydney. Her career took her to the four corners of the world and to the need to retain and promote the biblical faith amongst church people with widely different ideas. She was present of course at the birth of increasingly belligerent liberalism and was an observer at the last great Lambeth Conference in 1998 where these things came to a head.

How would you describe the ministry of this woman in her context?

I think you would need to say first of all that she was a teacher. Several people will mention her teaching skills. Thus, someone who was at Moore College in 1969 had Margaret as tutor. It was a significant step forward for Deaconess House and Margaret took the tutorial method she had seen at university and applied it at college. She got the students to write essays which were discussed and critiqued – not something that happened for most of the male students. I have been told how well it was done and with excellent results. Others have mentioned the one-to-one teaching they received.

Next, I would say that she was intellectually gifted. She researched, she spoke and wrote with considerable skill. Thus, in 1996, for example, she delivered one of the significant Halifax-Portal Lectures on the subject of 'The Ministry of Women', boldly observing, 'I am pleased to be part of this series, though the only woman lecturer. In our 1996 context, I find that a little dismaying. I am pleased to be speaking on my chosen topic. A seminal series without due consideration of one of the most pressing ecclesiastical issues of our time would have far less credibility'.[2] And she concludes, 'But it is finally not debate which wins supporters to acceptance of women's ministry. It is the genuine experience of women ministering in the congregation and amongst the people of God'.[3]

As I have already noted, had she wanted to go further into academic work, there is no doubt that she could have done so. Presumably her job at the General Synod office involved research, but I suspect it also involved the international elements to her career which I have already alluded to. Perhaps she was too busy doing good works to give years to academic work. I do not know.

Thirdly, I would say that she was a pioneer. At a time when few in Sydney were especially interested in ecumenical affairs or the Anglican Communion, she became deeply involved and her experiences helped mould her. She forged friendships and connections outside of our small world. She was prepared to engage in theological debates. She changed the direction of the education of women and the expectations that went with it. She advanced into the places which the next generation of women could and would go. She led the way, not least into the political life of the church and was never shy, not even if it may have made her unpopular at a time of considerable political turmoil over the role of women. Thus, people remember a powerful speech she made at

2 Margaret Rodgers, 'The Ministry of Women' in *A Real Yet Imperfect Communion: The 1996 and 1997 Halifax-Portal Lectures* (Strathfield: St Paul's Publications, 1998), 69.
3 Rodgers, 'The Ministry of Women', 85.

a conference in the mid-nineties held at Trinity Grammar School, a conference at which I, then Principal of Moore College, spoke for the other side.

I can guess who won that contest.

Her Person

But who was she as a person?

Let me remind you at this point that all I say is somewhat suppositional. Margaret was a friend and an important colleague, but not a close personal friend, and in this section in particular I may well be speaking out of turn. Nonetheless, let me at least raise the subject and begin the task of painting the portrait.

Despite the fact that she was a deaconess (and, interestingly, did not seek ordination to the diaconate), I did not think of Margaret as a parish worker as such. No doubt she would have done such a ministry very well. But her interests seemed other – in personality she was self-contained, not especially warm to colleagues, was not much prone to small-talk and did not suffer fools gladly. I don't mean she was not interested in other people or that she was selfish or egotistical, far from it. Indeed, she was kind. But she has also been described as feisty, and I guess that refers to the fact that she was never shy – no, not for a moment – in taking on any opposition in a debate. She fought with the best of them.

For some people, the wars they fight shape them forever. We can even become obsessive. Remember that I suggested that Margaret fought three battles – against ill-health, against restrictions on the ministry of women, against the secular world. It would have been very easy indeed for the struggle over the place of women to have dominated and obsessed her. But I think that it was the gospel of Jesus which held her heart first and foremost and that explains her best.

I say that as one who had the great privilege of working with her for six years in the media field. She was not trained for it. But that did not stop Margaret. She was working with a notoriously complementarian Archbishop. But that did not stop Margaret. Her knowledge, her skills, her loyalty, her strength were all at the service of the gospel and all put to the task of helping a hopeless amateur cope with the shark pool of world media. She remained the same fiesty, intelligent, savvy, experienced Margaret. One of my fondest memories is her comment to me after I was interviewed by a woman from the London Times: 'Peter, you are a sucker for a pretty face!'

That was Margaret.

Conclusion

There are eulogies and there is history. But the eulogies themselves are part of the history and so I have no hesitation in closing with part of my sermon at her funeral – for I was given the huge privilege of preaching on that occasion:

> I love the portrait of Margaret which adorns our service sheets today. The jacket is elegant. The award is rightly prominent and well-deserved. It gives you the chance to rejoice again as all her friends did. And the face is, to my mind, Margaret – smiling, quizzical, welcoming, and yet seeing into your very soul.
>
> Our lives intertwined over many years. Carillon Avenue, Abbotsleigh School and General Synod. Then there were the committees and synods of which she was so prominent a member, abounding in the work of the Lord. Even when we disagreed, we were allies because we sought the same things and served the same Lord. But, we were not merely colleagues – in fact I don't think Margaret would recognise that category in many of her relationships – we were friends, for she had the gift of friendship in abundance.
>
> Imagine my gratitude, then when Margaret continued her role as Media Officer after serving in that capacity during the time of Archbishop Goodhew. To say that the task was a difficult one would be to underestimate the challenges. How could we best promote the interests of Christ in a media world where ignorance was endemic, skepticism normal and opposition rife? Margaret was not trained for this role specifically. But she brought to it vital gifts which transcended any lacks.
>
> First, she was committed to Christ and his word. Second, she had the shrewdness which comes with spiritual wisdom. Third, she had very significant experience of the Anglican and Christian world beyond Sydney – the national church and the international church, especially Asia.

Fourth she was tough-minded and somewhat unflappable. Fifth, she had the loyalty which speaks its own mind. Sixth, with her capacity for friendship, she saw beyond the media as such and cultivated the people who work in the media. She introduced me to their world and helped me to move beyond merely stereotypical responses to what is said to relate to the actual people who are reporting our news. Seventh, she inducted me into the special role of the Archbishop in the community – a role which is hard to understand until you are actually in place. She helped me see the importance of justice for the poor and dispossessed. For all this and much more, I owe her my gratitude in a way which could never be fully recounted. I thank God for Margaret.

2. A brief history of the Deaconess Institute in Sydney
Colin Bale

My task is to write about the History of the Deaconess order in Sydney and then Margaret Rodgers as Principal of Deaconess House. The two parts are linked because of Margaret's research interest in deaconesses in the Church of England in the Diocese of Sydney and the beginning of that work.

Margaret Rodgers was a very able scholar. She received a Licentiate in Theology with First Class Honours from the Australian College of Theology in 1963. She was also awarded the Deaconess House Diploma in the same year. She completed a Bachelor of Arts from the University of Sydney in 1970, the same year she was made a deaconess by the Archbishop of Sydney. In 1977, she was awarded a Bachelor of Divinity with Honours from the University of Sydney. She also received the Rachel McKibbin Prize, which was awarded to the best candidate in Ecclesiastical History Year IV Honours. Her honours thesis was 'Deaconesses in the Church of England in the Nineteenth Century: with special attention to the early years of 'Bethany' Church of England Deaconess Institution, Sydney, New South Wales'. I have read Margaret's thesis and it is a fine piece of scholarship. Indeed, I utilise some of her research and writing to explain how the Deaconess Institution was established in Sydney in the late nineteenth century.

In the last two decades of the nineteenth century in Sydney there arose the question of whether women should be involved in formal Anglican ministry and, if so, what shape this should take. In 1885, the Synod of the Anglican Diocese of Sydney appointed a select committee to report on the ministry of women in the Diocese. The committee was asked to 'consider the advisability of organising the religious and charitable ministry of women in this diocese'.[1] As a result of the committee's work, two motions from the committee were tabled at the Synod:

1. That this Synod adopts the report of the select committee on the ministry of women so far as the same relates to the employment of deaconesses in this diocese.

---

[1] Nora Tress, *Caught for Life: A Story of the Anglican Deaconess Order in Australia* (Araluen, N.S.W.: N. Tress, 1993), 22.

2. That it is undesirable to establish a sisterhood in the diocese.[2]

In the Synod, it was clear that the majority would favour deaconesses but were opposed to the introduction of a sisterhood.[3] To the Synod the idea of a sisterhood was unattractive because it was linked to Anglo-Catholicism and its attendant ritualism. Yet, while the recommendation about deaconesses was viewed positively, it wasn't implemented by the diocese. When it did happen a few years later it was independent of the Synod and thus outside Synod control.

The movement to have deaconesses in the Anglican Diocese of Sydney had its beginnings with the Bethanien Deaconess Institute in Stettin, Germany. The Rev Mervyn Archdall, a Sydney clergyman, had married Martha Karow, the daughter of a Lutheran pastor at Stettin. Mrs Archdall was familiar with Bethanien as it was not far from where she had grown up.[4] The beginnings of the training and ministry of deaconesses in Sydney were very modest. Rev Archdall sought support from fellow clergy and was given great encouragement by Rev J D Langley, Rector of St Philip's Church, Sydney. He was later to be the Bishop of Bendigo.

With a small group of supporters, Archdall established a deaconess institution in Sydney. Miss Menia Maspero, who received her training at the London Deaconess Institution, was appointed as the first Deaconess Superintendent. Rev Archdall informed the Archbishop of Sydney that the establishment of deaconesses in Sydney therefore 'had a double link ... from Bethanien, via London, and owed something to both sources of origin'.[5]

Margaret Rodgers says of the establishment of the Bethany Deaconess Institution in Sydney that it was mostly the creation of Mervyn and Martha Archdall, and it 'did not arise out of any active feminist agitation in the Church of England in Sydney ... Women did not commence the work.'[6] Although first wave feminism was active at the time Bethany

2 Tress, *Caught for Life*, 22.
3 Margaret Rodgers, *Deaconesses in the Church of England in the Nineteenth Century: with Special Attention to the Early Years of 'Bethany' Church of England Deaconess Institution, Sydney, New South Wales* (Unpublished BD thesis, University of Sydney, 1977), 129.
4 Deaconess Institution, *The Vision Unfolding: Deaconess Institution, 1891–1991*, 6.
5 *The Vision Unfolding*, 7.
6 Rodgers, *Deaconesses in the Church of England*, 131.

was established and this women's movement led to the creation of organisations like the Women's Christian Temperance Union, it was not the case that the move for deaconesses in the Diocese of Sydney actively arose from the feminist movement. Moreover, as Margaret Rodgers makes clear in her thesis, 'the men who were the creators of the scheme and their supporters in the church at large held a very conservative view of the place of women in the church and society'.[7] Indeed, no woman was a member of the council of Bethany for the first eighteen years.[8]

The other important thing to note about the establishment of the Bethany Church of England Deaconess Institution is that it was created independently of the Archbishop and Synod of the Diocese of Sydney, and this was the situation from then onwards. While there were generally good relations with successive archbishops, and they were usually supportive of the Institution, there was no legal governance of it exercised by either the diocesan bishop or diocesan Synod.

Thus established, how did the Deaconess Institution fare?

Bethany began in 1891 at Balmain. It later moved to Redfern, then Lewisham and Darlington, before finishing at Queen Street, Newtown in 1916. That was the training location of the Deaconess Institution from then onwards. Women from middle class or well-to-do families were seen as the most likely candidates for Bethany. However, only a few women applied in the first few years.[9] That was disappointing and Deaconess Katherine Nickolls, who was Head Deaconess, suggested that a significant reason for this was that 'some women consider it beneath their social position to give themselves to the work of a Deaconess.'[10] She went on to assert that although there was probably a decline in social standing for a woman becoming a deaconess, 'what is the loss of the social distinctions of the world in comparison with the honour of serving the King of Kings?'[11] In an article in an earlier issue of *The Deaconess*, the Head Deaconess made it clear that the 'regime' for deaconesses in training was usually austere and highly regulated,

---

7 Rodgers, *Deaconesses in the Church of England*, 132.
8 Rodgers, *Deaconesses in the Church of England*, 132.
9 Rodgers, *Deaconesses in the Church of England*, 111.
10 *The Deaconess*, 30 September 1896, 4.
11 *The Deaconess*, 30 September 1896, 4.

and explains why it may not have been very attractive to the type of young Christian women the Institute hoped to enrol.[12]

The number of deaconesses trained in Sydney over the years was never large. Between 1901 and 1913 only fifteen women became deaconesses in Sydney.[13] Nora Tress in her book, *Caught for Life: A Story of the Anglican Deaconess Order in Australia,* states that there were 132 women trained as deaconesses in Australia from 1891 to 1991. Of that number, the greater majority were trained in Sydney. The last deaconess was 'set apart', or formally commissioned, in Sydney in 1991.[14]

The first two deaconesses trained at Bethany were set apart at St. Andrew's Cathedral, Sydney in September 1893.[15] The service for the 'Making of Deaconesses' made it clear what ministry would be like for them:

> to aid in all spiritual ministrations except public services of the church, to assist in all such good works as shall be committed unto her, to nurse the sick, to visit and relieve the poor and the afflicted, to tend and instruct the young and ignorant; to minister especially to women who need to be brought to the grace and service of God; and in all things to help the minister of Christ in any parish in which she may be appointed to serve.[16]

The ministry of deaconesses largely followed that form for the next 100 years.

Over the years the Deaconess Institution established schools, nursing homes and hospitals in which deaconesses could minister. As well, the ministry of Deaconess House broadened to include women undertaking theological studies but not intending to be deaconesses, and female university boarders. By the 1960s many women entering Deaconess House to study were married before they were set apart, or married soon after, and did not work as deaconesses.[17]

---

12 *The Deaconess,* 19 January 1895, 6.
13 Anne O'Brien, *God's Willing Workers* (Sydney: UNSW Press, 2005), 99.
14 Anglican Deaconess Ministries, 'The Deaconesses', https://www.deaconessministries.org.au/meet-our-deaconesses.
15 Tress, *Caught for Life,* 24.
16 Tress, *Caught for life,* 25.
17 O'Brien, *God's willing workers,* 118.

3. The principalship of Margaret Rodgers at Deaconess House 1976–1985

Colin Bale

Before turning to consider Margaret Rodgers' term as Principal of Deaconess House, let me set the context by saying a little about her predecessor Mary Andrews. In 1975 Deaconess Mary Andrews retired as Principal of Deaconess House. Mary Andrews is something of a legendary and resolute figure. She had been both Head Deaconess of the Deaconess Institute, and Principal of Deaconess House. She had held these positions since 1952. One of her students described Deaconess Andrews as a 'loving but firm director'.[1] The term 'firm' connotes her determination, particularly to maintain the best traditions of Deaconess House. Although she had abundant energy, holding both roles meant that she was heavily involved not only in the training of women at Deaconess House but in the administration and operation of many aspects of the Deaconess Institution. She was on the boards of the Deaconess Institution, the Home of Peace Hospitals, the Braeside Church of England Hospital, the Lisgar House Management Committee, Hilsyde Management Committee, as well as the Deaconess House Management Committee.[2] That list of responsibilities does not take into account her diocesan roles or involvement in other organisations.

Margaret Rodgers replaced Mary Andrews as the Principal in 1976. Mary Andrews, however, remained Head Deaconess until December 1982, splitting the roles of Head Deaconess and Principal. They continued to be split when Jean Stanfield became Head Deaconess in 1982. This meant that Margaret Rodgers was able to focus particularly on Deaconess House, without significant calls on her time from the other ministries of the Deaconess Institute.

What qualifications and experience made Margaret Rodgers a suitable candidate for Principal? She had been made a deaconess in 1970 by the Archbishop of Sydney. She had been a tutor and an assistant to the Principal at Deaconess House from 1969 to 1973. She was the Warden of the Church of England Women's Hall, Sydney in 1974 and 1975. Thus, she was very familiar with the operation of

1 Hayley Lukabyo, 'Who was Mary Andrews?', https://www.deaconessministries.org.au/news/who-was-mary-andrews.
2 Deaconess Institute Report 1975, 20.

Deaconess House and her role as the Warden of the Women's Hall meant that she had had some executive and leadership experience. In both places she had exercised a pastoral role. Her obvious academic ability, touched on before, meant that she was well placed to lead Deaconess House in encouraging women to undertake rigorous ministry training.

Margaret Rodgers was very keen for women to be well-trained for gospel ministry. In the report of her first full year as principal, she was able to note an increase in the number of Deaconess House students. There were nineteen students enrolled, with eleven women enrolling in First Year.[3] There was also a full complement of boarders. In 1980 Margaret Rodgers reported that the first-year group was the largest in many years.[4] The total number of students enrolled was twenty-nine. In 1983 there were twenty-nine women enrolled in either the Bachelor of Theology or Diploma of Bible and Missions, both courses run by Moore Theological College. Yet, it was about more than numbers of students. She wanted to see more women undertake more rigorous theological and pastoral study. Narelle Jarrett, her successor as Principal, said that Margaret in her time as Principal challenged many women to tackle the Bachelor of Theology degree.[5] Narelle also noted that she encouraged this by her own scholarly example, notably her completion of the Bachelor of Divinity (Honours) at the University of Sydney in 1977.[6]

She made it clear that she wanted to introduce change at Deaconess House. Some of the changes she made indicated a generational shift. The uniforms worn by students prior to her appointment were done away with. Mealtimes became less formal and food choices more attractive. She was more open, for pastoral reasons, to deaconess candidates living away from Deaconess House if there were good reasons to do so.

As the Principal of Deaconess House, she was a member of the Moore College Faculty. She was a very capable teacher and delivered lectures in modern church history. Narelle Jarrett wrote that Margaret won the respect of her Moore College peers and students

---

3 Deaconess House Report 1977, 4-5.
4 Deaconess House Report 1980, 5.
5 Deaconess House Report 1985, 4.
6 Deaconess House Report 1985, 4.

for her 'teaching ability, her capacity to analyse and her ability in discussion'.[7]

New initiatives at Deaconess House were undertaken during her principalship. New courses of study were offered to the students. For example, she introduced a course focused on mission studies.[8] As well, regular in-service seminars were organised for women working as deaconesses or parish sisters. Ex-student reunions were established, and this resulted in the Ex-Students Fellowship. She was also keen for people to know something of the calibre of women training at Deaconess House, so brief profiles of some students were included in the newsletters.[9]

While Principal of Deaconess House, Margaret Rodgers took the opportunity to be involved in national and international conferences and consultations. Some of these were: the Australian Anglican Deaconess Conference; Anglican Delegate to the Australian Council of Churches; member of the Partners in Mission Consultation of the Anglican Church of Australia; Delegate to the World Council of Churches; Conference on World Mission and Evangelism, Lausanne Consultation. Margaret began to have a media presence. She was a participant in the 'Interfaith Service: Turning Toward Peace' that was broadcast on ABC television in September 1982.[10] The other key participants were the Dalai Lama, Rabbi Brian Fox, Chief Minister of Temple Emanuel, and Bishop Bede Heather, Catholic diocesan bishop of Parramatta.

As Principal, Deaconess Rodgers was involved in diocesan discussions about the role of women in ministry. She was a member of the Archbishop's Committee to study the 'Theology of Ordination'.[11] She said that it was hoped the report 'will be received as a significant contribution to the life and ministry of the Diocese'.[12] Her successor as Principal, Narelle Jarrett, said that Margaret had represented the work of women in the diocese well and had 'done much to encourage progress towards opening the Order of Deacons to women.'[13]

---

7 Deaconess House Report, 1986, 4.
8 Deaconess House Report 1980, 5.
9 Deaconess House Report, 1979, 6.
10 *Australian Jewish Times*, 2 September 1982, 23.
11 Deaconess House Report, 1979, 6.
12 Deaconess House Report, 1979, 6.
13 Deaconess House Report, 1986, 4.

Much of what I have said thus far has been taken from written sources, particularly the Report of Deaconess House by the Principal in the Annual Report of the Deaconess Institute. But what was Margaret Rodgers like as the Principal? Thanks to the efforts of Jacinth Myles and Jan Donohoo, who kindly contacted some of the women who were at Deaconess House in Margaret's time, I was able to hear from these women about Margaret and what she was like. Here are some excerpts:

- Rev[14] Daphne May has vivid memories of the vast improvement in the food served, when Margaret became principal. Daphne also remembers Margaret's encouragement for students to preach in the Deaconess House chapel and the careful, helpful feedback she then gave each student. Daphne graduated in 1976.

- Rev Lu (Lucille) Piper was a Church Army sister, working at St Luke's Mosman. In 1989, when Margaret came to speak on deputation at a neighbouring church, Lu went along to listen to her. Margaret asked Lu if she had been asked by the then Archbishop Donald Robinson about being ordained to the diaconate (the first group of Sydney women were ordained in February 1989). Lu hadn't been asked and was subsequently knocked back when she did apply. However, after what Lu called a tortuous path, she eventually was ordained in 1991. Lu regarded Margaret's initial question and subsequent encouragement as directed by God.

- Rev Diane Jeffree remembers Margaret as an excellent tutor at Deaconess House and as a woman of compassion and understanding. Diane also commented that Margaret was at the forefront of introducing changes, including better food (no more 1.5 sausages every Monday night) and modern uniforms. These relatively superficial changes were appreciated by the students and were an indication of a more substantive movement from the archaic to the contemporary.

- Rev Marcia Green also recalls Margaret's keen mind and academic rigor as tutor, as well as being very patient. Marcia recalled that she often saw Margaret as she prepared to leave for Diocesan meetings, always smartly attired and very well

14 The title Reverend denotes the women who were later ordained deacon in the Anglican Church.

organised with all her materials ready and accessible. Marcia said Margaret was well prepared to meet them on their turf.

- Helen Plumb remembers Margaret as a great encourager to keep going in her studies and Christian service.

- Karen Watt (nee Lovell) not only has fond memories of Margaret, but regards her as one of the wise women. Her experience was that Margaret encouraged her to take up a position at Macquarie University School of Christian Studies as a tutor. This meant Karen would have to leave Deaconess House as a resident, whilst still being a Moore College student. There were strict rules about female students living at the College, but Margaret saw the advantage to Karen and was prepared to 'break the rules' for the benefit of others.

- Rev Janis Donohoo (nee Smith) thought Margaret was a fascinating character, one not easily defined nor pigeonholed. She had a wry sense of humour, was meticulous about schedules and self-discipline, was loyal to her rugby league team (Newtown Jets, Balmain Tigers, or Wests Magpies...) and loved classical poetry. She tutored Janis over the first year summer break when she had to re-sit her Greek exam and was quietly despairing when Janis didn't do the work Margaret had set. She treated Janis as an adult and didn't harangue, but when Janis got the message and passed with good marks. Margaret was pleased. She was not one for extravagances, but nor was she mean. She was generous with her time and the resources she had to offer. Margaret invited Janis to accompany her to meet with a delegation from the Three-Self Church movement of China. It was a rather bizarre event and Margaret was poised and confident, but not unaware. Janis thinks this was typical of the woman. She was not Machiavellian but she also knew the realities of her situation within the diocese and particularly, Moore College. She was astute, fair and no fool. [15]

That gives us a glimpse of Margaret the Principal from the students' perspective.

---

[15] This information has been checked and authorised by the contributors, previous students of Deaconess House when Deaconess Margaret Rodgers was tutor and then Principal.

In February 1985 Margaret Rodgers resigned as Principal of Deaconess House. She had held the position for almost ten years. Narelle Jarrett penned a fitting tribute. She spoke of the depth of Margaret's contribution to the ministry of Deaconess House, Moore Theological College, and the Anglican Diocese of Sydney, stating that she was 'a godly example' to those in ministry training, 'respected for her untiring work and service', and 'her clear-headedness regarding theological issues'.[16]

Apart from the assessment of Margaret Rodgers' principalship given by Narelle Jarrett in 1985, there doesn't seem to be any other detailed appraisal of Margaret Rodgers' time at Deaconess House that I could find. In Nora Tress's book about deaconesses in Australia published in 1993, the focus was primarily on deaconesses in Sydney and provided some brief biographies of significant deaconesses. Margaret Rodgers was not included. Reading through the biographies I concluded that perhaps the reason why is that she never matched the 'norm' of a typical deaconess. She hadn't been formally involved with a nursing home, hospital, or children's home. Although a keen parishioner in her local church, she had never been a parish sister. Indeed, the path she chose after resigning as Principal of Deaconess House in 1985, was not typical. She took up the position as Administration and Research Officer for the General Synod of the Anglican Church of Australia, a position well-suited to her abilities and interests, but not one that matched the expected pathways for a deaconess.

So, what to say about her as Principal? Very able, intellectually bright, willing to make changes that she thought were appropriate, flexible when needed, a great encourager, setting high expectations for students, yet patient and kind. Above all she was committed to serving the Lord Jesus by utilising the gifts he had given her in ministering to the women under her care so that they were well-equipped for Gospel ministry.

---

16 Deaconess House Report, 1986, 4.

4. Margaret Rodgers – Serving the Diocese through Synod and Standing Committee

Kara Hartley

On Tuesday 18 October 2011, the following motion was presented to the Sydney Synod:

Synod Motion 6.9

Deaconess Margaret Rodgers

Synod gives thanks to God for the ministry of Deaconess Margaret Rodgers, who retired from Synod last year, and in particular –

(a) her distinguished presence on the floor of Synod for over thirty years;

(b) her longstanding membership of Standing Committee (since 1982);

(c) her service to the General Synod as a diocesan representative since 1979, serving on both its Standing Committee and international committees, including her time as General Synod Research Officer (1985–1993);

(d) her commitment to the training of women in ministry through Deaconess House, as Tutor, Vice-Principal and finally Principal from 1976–1985;

(e) her professional expertise in media relations, becoming the first CEO of Anglican Media (1994–2003) and then the Archbishop's Media Officer (2004–2007); and

(f) her unwavering commitment to Christ in the service of others for over forty years as a Deaconess.

Synod expresses its gratitude to Margaret and wishes her God's blessing upon her future life and ministry.

(Dr Karin Sowada/Bishop Glenn Davies)[1]

---

1 Anglican Diocese of Sydney Synod, Proceedings of the 49th Synod, 2011, 32/11, 34.

This motion summarises the contribution of one of the key women in the life of the diocese in the many different spheres of governance and oversight she moved in, not only in the diocese of Sydney, but across the national church.

I remember meeting with Margaret when she was Media Officer for the Archbishop. It was my first meeting with her, as my time as a Meriden [Anglican School] girl didn't overlap with her years teaching there!

The year was 2007 and I was writing a church history essay on the training of women in the Sydney Diocese in the 1960s. Margaret had completed her diploma of Theology with first class honours at Deaconess House in 1963, before going on to study a Bachelor of Arts from the University of Sydney. She had been tutor and assistant to the Principal of Deaconess House in 1969–1972 before becoming Principal herself in 1976.

She knew a thing or two about the training of women in our diocese. I don't remember much of that meeting apart from being very nervous in the presence of such an accomplished and able woman.

Yet while she held an unwavering commitment to women being trained and deployed in ministry across the diocese, she was also clearly skilled in leadership through committee work. I don't know if she enjoyed it, but the number of committees on which she served surely meant she had some kind of natural inclination to contributing this way.

Margaret's involvement in the governance and life of the diocese and national church is extraordinary. There are few, apart from perhaps our most senior lay leaders, who have served in such extensive ways.

It's worth considering her service in full.

Local Church, Appointment to Synod and Standing Committee

As she began her leadership at Deaconess House as Principal she also joined the Sydney Synod, as a lay representative of the Newtown parish. It is unclear if she began her time on Synod in 1976 or 1977, as she was elected to replace another member who was originally elected to serve in the 1975–1977 triennium. She remained on Synod until 2011, some 35 years. I confess I'm not sure I aspire to be a member for that long.

Throughout her time as a Synod representative she also stood and was elected as both Church Warden and parish councillor of the parish of Newtown/Erskineville. She only finished on parish council a year before her death. Upon her death, in an article written for the diocesan magazine Southern Cross, Bishop Glenn Davies mentioned that the local church was of vital importance for Margaret,[2] beyond just attending to governance matters.

Dr David Hohne, member of the Moore College faculty and long-term member of Newtown parish remembers her ability to 'dissect' the sermons of young student ministers from Moore College! Her theological mind always applied to the training and formation of future ministers.[3]

Synod and Standing Committee

While Margaret would have been one of several women at Synod, but still significantly in the minority, her election to Standing Committee made her the first woman to participate in this arena. The motion made at her retirement indicated she joined Standing Committee in 1982. However, she was nominated in November of 1978 and from the Standing Committee minutes, her first meeting was 1979. She remained on that committee until 2011. In many ways that fact is extremely important in understanding Margaret's place in the diocese. The phrase 'a woman in a man's world' seems totally apt at this point.

Bishop Glenn Davies recalls Deaconess Rodgers certainly 'held her own' among the cut and thrust of debate in the Standing Committee. He also recalls that Margaret used the fact that she was in the minority as a woman to her advantage often by starting her speeches saying, 'I know I'm only a woman but ...' or words to that effect. He says, 'She was a formidable speaker in Synod. Her speeches carried weight. She understood Synod procedure and used it to her advantage.'[4] Dr Robert Tong said, 'she certainly wasn't backward in coming forward'.[5]

Of course, the man's world she inhabited was a thoroughly Christian, gospel-hearted and minded group, but doesn't discount the need for

2 Russell Powell, 'Prominent Deaconess dies', *Sydney Anglicans* 31 May 2014, https://sydneyanglicans.net/news/prominent-deaconess-dies.
3 Written comment sent to the author.
4 Written comment sent to the author.
5 Comment made verbally to the author.

a woman in this context to have a particular strength of character and mind. It appears from all reports that Deaconess Rodgers was both highly capable and a keen contributor in debates.

Dr Karin Sowada, who was the CEO of the Anglican Deaconess Institution from 2008–2015, says in her article in the Sydney Morning Herald, July 2014: 'Early on, Rodgers was often the only woman in a room of men but she was not intimidated. Indeed, her very presence opened the door for many to follow.'[6]

For the next section, I want to focus on the contributions Margaret made in Synod.

The Doctrine Commission

I believe one of the most significant groups working in the diocese is the doctrine commission. With about 10 members this group meets each month to prepare theological papers in response to issues referred to it by Synod or the Archbishop.

In fact, it was Margaret who moved the motion at Synod in 1981 to establish the commission. The motion read,

> 19/81 Diocesan Doctrine Commission
>
> Synod requests the Archbishop, in consultation with the Standing Committee, to appoint a Diocesan Doctrine Commission, to consider and report on issues which may be referred to from time to time by the Synod, the Standing Committee, or by boards and committees set up by the Synod. The Commission to be comprised of ten persons.
>
> (Deaconess MA Rodgers, 8.10.81)[7]

As we noted earlier, she graduated with distinction from her theological studies which made her suitably qualified to be appointed as one of the founding members of the doctrine commission in 1983, serving for 10 years.

---

6 Karin Sowada, 'Deaconess was key in training women for ministry', *Sydney Morning Herald,* July 16, 2014, https://www.smh.com.au/national/deaconess-was-key-in-training-woman-for-ministry-20140716-ztiyy.html (accessed 26 February 2024).
7 Year Book of the Diocese of Sydney, 1982, 255.

During her time, the commission produced reports on the ordination of women, re-marriage of divorced people, the ministry of women and diaconal presidency to name just a few.

To suggest these were somewhat significant issues for the doctrine commission to consider would be putting it lightly. As we know, the ordination of women to the diaconate took place in the Sydney Diocese in 1989, right in the middle of Margaret's time on the commission. Despite the 1989 ruling, Margaret did not pursue this herself, happy to remain a deaconess all her life.

While Margaret's name was the one beside the motion, it would be true to say that the idea for the commission was probably not hers alone. As often happens with these kinds of things at Synod, a mover of a motion would have been in discussion with others, likely in this case the Archbishop of the day, or the Principal of Moore College or other significant people in the diocese.

Over her time in Synod Deaconess Rodgers moved 20 motions. Not all were controversial or of great significance – such as the motion respectfully asking the Archbishop of the day to send Christian greetings from the Synod to Archbishop Sir Marcus Loane, on the occasion of his 92nd birthday or the question she asked about whether there was a more expedient way to handle questions and answers at Synod.

Or the motion she moved in 1980 which has affected my life as a Synod member: That standing orders be changed so Synod didn't meet before 3.15pm and ordinances not taken before 4.30pm.[8]

But other motions betrayed a deep sense of Deaconess Rodgers' commitment to good and significant areas of social justice.

These include:

- Opposition to the opening of the Sydney Harbour Casino

- Opposition to euthanasia legislation (1996)

- Production of materials to enhance connections between Christians and those in the cross cultural and indigenous communities (2000)

---

8 Year Book of the Diocese of Sydney, 1981, 243.

- Prayers for the end of violence in Israel, Jerusalem and the West Bank

- Opposition to embryonic stem cell research

- The war in Iraq

- Care of people with disabilities

Holy Communion

Two motions concerning the administration of holy communion were moved by Margaret. The first was in 1990, in response to comments from Archbishop Robinson's presidential address.

The other was in 1993 when she and Bishop Glenn Davies were the catalysts for the Doctrine Commission report which would re-examine the issue of whether children should be permitted to receive Holy Communion before they were confirmed, and if so to then decide whether the diocese would be willing to adopt the General Synod canon relating to this matter which the Synod had previously declined to adopt.

In 1997 the canon was adopted despite the fact the Doctrine Commission was not overwhelmingly swayed by the article Glenn Davies had written for the Reformed Theological Review.[9]

Women in Ministry

The final area of Margaret's work on Synod that I want to focus on is a couple of motions around women in ministry. I'll take them in chronological order.

Each betray a deep concern and conviction about the place of women in the Diocese.

Firstly,

> 34/77 Superannuation for Parish Sisters
>
> That Synod requests Standing Committee to consider the position of parish sisters who are licensed in the Diocese in relation to the Sydney Diocesan Superannuation Fund,

---

9 Glenn N. Davies, 'The Lord's Supper for the Lord's Children', *Reformed Theological Review*, 50.1, (Jan – Apr 1991): 12-20.

with a view to making it mandatory for contributions to be made by parishes in which they serve.

(Deaconess MA Rodgers – 10.10.1977)[10]

Parish Sisters were lay women serving in formal ministry in the diocese. They are licenced but back in the 1970s they weren't part of compulsory superannuation contributions.

This is clearly a motion that seeks to support these women and ensure that provision is made for their future. The diocese had legislated superannuation for clergy since 1906 and then in 1961 an ordinance broadened the provisions to other workers including deaconesses. Yet Parish Sisters, women who were also licenced in the diocese, weren't included. Records show this motion was passed and an amendment was made to the ordinance the following year to include Parish Sisters.

Secondly, in 2008 Margaret moved a motion honouring the ministries done by women in the diocese.

I don't think there was anything in particular going on for women at that time. Narelle Jarrett had just begun full time as the Archdeacon for Women's Ministry.

So really this seems to be a call to arms in many ways, to continue considering how to raise up and deploy women for ministry.

7/08   Ministry of women in the Diocese

Synod acknowledges and gives thanks to God for the creative and God-honouring ministry of women in the Diocese of Sydney at this time and over many years, including lay women in parishes, licensed lay workers, pastoral workers, clergy wives, chaplains and ordained deacons.

Synod also gives thanks for the numbers of women training and preparing for ministry through Moore College with the support of the Anglican Deaconess Institution Sydney Limited (ADISL) as well as Mary Andrews College, Youthworks College and the Department of Ministry Training and Development.

---

10 Year Book of the Diocese of Sydney, 1978, 248–249.

Synod further requests parish leaders to encourage many other mature and gifted women members to undertake theological and ministry training to enhance their contribution to the ministry of the Gospel throughout the Diocese and beyond.

(Deaconess Margaret Rodgers 14/10/08)[11]

While Margaret was leading this motion, what we're missing as we read these excerpts from the minutes of Synod and Standing Committee is her voice.

We don't have recordings of the speeches which accompanied these motions, the sense of urging or pleading which supported the hopes and desires of the motion.

As I mentioned earlier, Margaret's time on these bodies was at the height of debates and decisions regarding women's ordination. During her time on the doctrine commission several reports were produced in relation to this matter.

Additionally, while we have access to all the motions Margaret moved in Synod, we don't have a record as to how often, and on what, she spoke in Synod. All I can do is picture Synod and imagine her standing in her place waiting for the call from the President. From those I've spoken to who were there I get a sense that when Margaret stood it was a brave Archbishop to ignore her and not give her the nod to go ahead.

Perhaps some will be able to recall she was a consistent contributor on all sorts of debates, not just the ones she was promoting.

Beyond the Synod

Deaconess Rodgers was also Chief Executive Officer (CEO) of the Anglican Media Council from 1994 to 2003, her final official 'job' in the diocese before retirement.

Karin Sowada suggests that the way Deaconess Rodgers understood the political nature of the diocese, and how the various groups within the diocese worked, made her a trusted advisor to many in leadership.[12]

---

11 Diocese of Sydney Synod, Resolutions 2008, https://www.sds.asn.au/session-Synod-resolutions-2008 (accessed 27 February 2024).
12 Sowada, 'Deaconess was key in training women for ministry', SMH.

Glenn Davies reflects, 'When she became CEO of Anglican Media (the first female CEO of a diocesan organisation) under Harry Goodhew, she became more and more influential in Standing Committee, Synod, General Synod Standing Committee and General Synod. She then became Peter Jensen's media officer and was superb in that role, protecting Peter and the diocese, and promoting the gospel in the public sphere.'[13]

The National Church

After her time in leadership at Deaconess House in 1985, Deaconess Rodgers became the research officer for the General Synod Office, beginning a long career of service in the wider Anglican Church.

She had joined the General Synod in 1979, also serving on the Standing Committee from that year so she was familiar with the challenges, opportunities and tensions facing the national church.

She remained on General Synod Standing Committee until 2000 and the General Synod until 2010. Once again, she participated in significant theological work through the General Synod Doctrine Commission.

From Glenn Davies, "Margaret was an able historian and researcher, writing for ACL [Anglican Church League] and other publications. It was not surprising that she became the Research Officer for General Synod."[14]

Yet while much of her service was on larger stages of Synods and Standing Committees, or contribution to the theological considerations of significant matters, much of her board and committee work was unseen.

The years of toil and conversations and debates are now locked away, reflected in the minutes and agendas of various meetings for various bodies around the diocese, the nation and overseas.

For example, as Karin Sowada outlines in her article, Margaret was a board member and chairwoman of New College, of the University of NSW, board member of World Vision (1999 to 2008) and director of Anglican Deaconess Ministries. She also served on the World Vision board from 1999 to 2008 and was an Anglican representative of the National Council of Churches of Australia from 1994 to 2007.[15]

---

13 Written comment sent to the author.
14 Written comment sent to the author.
15 Sowada, 'Deaconess was key in training women for ministry', SMH.

Idleness does not seem to be a word in the lexicon of Margaret Rodgers.

Final Words

The final clauses of the motion presented to the 2011 Synod say,

> Synod, giving thanks, for:
>
> her unwavering commitment to Christ in the service of others for over forty years as a Deaconess.
>
> Synod expresses its gratitude to Margaret and wishes her God's blessing upon her future life and ministry.[16]

For all the years of recording minutes, sitting in committee meetings, listening and contributing to debates, listening to those she agreed and disagreed with, Margaret was known for her unwavering commitment to Christ.

It was her Lord she was serving as she joined committees and served on boards. Her calling as a Deaconess and her obvious leadership skills allowed her to participate in significant ways guiding the activities of the diocese and guarding the gospel.

So many today spurn the idea of contributing at this level but in fact we need people who have sound gospel convictions to offer themselves for this work, sacrificially, as Deaconess Rodgers was willing to do.

Global ministry

Globally, she was a representative on the Anglican Consultative Council (1990, 1996, 1999, 2002) and attended the Lambeth Conference of Anglican bishops in 1998.

She served as joint president of the Christian Conference of Asia 1995–2000, and was an observer of the World Council of Churches.

While for many people serving in this kind of way sounds dry and life sapping, it is clear Margaret not only had the right skills for such work, willingness to contribute in this way, but also understood the significance of participation and leadership in this way of service.

---

16 Anglican Diocese of Sydney Synod, Proceedings of the 49th Synod, 2011, 32/11, 34.

5. 'Extracurricular activities' - The ecumenical service of Deaconess Margaret Rodgers AM

Rod Benson

In a motion to the General Synod of the Anglican Church of Australia on 1 July 2014, referring to the late Deaconess Margaret Rodgers AM, Dr Robert Tong AM observed that 'Margaret's extensive 'extracurricular' activities were largely undertaken in Margaret's own time, during periods of annual leave or in some instances where her employer decided it would be beneficial for all concerned for Margaret to be involved as 'part of her employment'.[1] It is my pleasure to comment on some of those 'extracurricular' activities.

Introduction

By all accounts, Margaret Rodgers (1939–2014) was an extraordinary gift of God to the Anglican Church. For some years, I worked with Margaret on the executive of the NSW Council of Churches; I succeeded her as writer and broadcaster of the Council's 'Sunday editorials' on Sydney radio station 2CH; and I had the honour of writing the entry on Margaret's life and work in the second edition of the *Australian Dictionary of Evangelical Biography*.[2] In the *ADEB* article, I said:

> Developing a reputation as kind and intelligent, with keen historical and theological judgment, a dry wit, and common sense, Rodgers was ordained a deaconess of the Anglican Church in 1970. Disinclined to pursue ordination as a priest, which would necessitate leaving the Sydney Diocese, she nevertheless rose to become one of the most powerful lay leaders in the Diocese.

In 1994, Rodgers was appointed chief executive officer of Anglican Media, serving the Sydney Diocese, where she remained until 2003. In this role, she transformed the diocesan newspaper, *Southern Cross*, into a free monthly magazine with a circulation of 40,000 and significantly strengthened the Diocese's media profile. She wrote a regular column for *Southern Cross*, penning articles ranging from a critique of the theology of Pope Benedict XVI to a commentary on the morality of the

---

1 Resolution 35/14, seconded by Dr Karin Sowada.
2 Benson, "Margaret Amelia Rodgers", ADEB .

fashion industry. From 2004–2007, she was Archbishop Peter Jensen's media officer. [3]

Margaret's scholarship reflects her passion for Anglicanism and her desire for greater recognition of the contribution of women in the church. Her 1977 Bachelor of Divinity (Honours) thesis, submitted to the University of Sydney, presents a history of deaconesses in the Church of England in the nineteenth century with special reference to the early years of Bethany Church of England Deaconess Institution, Sydney. Various publications on related themes followed.[4]

Margaret served as a member of the Synod of the Anglican Diocese of Sydney from 1976–2011, at times being the only woman elected. In 1978, she was the first woman elected to the Synod's Standing Committee. In her 1996 Halifax-Portal Lecture, the inaugural series of this ecumenical venture, on 'The ministry of women,' Margaret remarked that she found it 'a little dismaying' to be the only woman lecturer.[5]

Her keen intellect, forthrightness, and theological formation were early evident, such as when she negotiated with Archbishop Marcus Loane the terms of her Institution Service as Principal of Deaconess House. In a letter to Archbishop Loane dated 8 December 1975, Margaret writes:

> For some time I have been uneasy about the service presently used at the Institution of Deaconesses and Parish Sisters in the Diocese ... In its present form I find the Service repetitive, rambling, sentimental and possessing no liturgical merit. When I read it I am unable to isolate any underlying doctrine of ministry upon which it rests, and it seems to me to sit very uneasily within the context of the liturgy which surrounds it. If you are happy with the idea, I would like to suggest that perhaps Alan Blanch,

3 Benson, "Margaret Amelia Rodgers", ADEB.
4 For example, 'In Sydney – Deaconesses or Sisters? The coming of the Kilburn sisters,' *Australian Church Record*, 15 Dec 1980, 1, 8; 'Deaconesses and the Diaconate: An Anglican debate,' *St. Mark's Review*, Dec 1980, 38–47; 'The Ministry of omen,' in Ewan Donald Cameron et al, *A Real Yet Imperfect Communion: The 1996 and 1997 Halifax-Portal Lectures* (Strathfield, NSW: St Paul's Publications, 1998), 69–86.
5 Rodgers, "The Ministry of Women," 69.

Peter Jensen and myself could design an alternate service, and submit it to you for your approval.[6]

Archbishop Loane was happy with the idea, and an alternate service was approved.

Media work

These qualities served Margaret well in the male-oriented and ideologically charged world of the Sydney Diocese. They also served her well in the combative secular media world. The Diocese proposed various plans to make better use of print, radio and television media to promote the gospel message and the Anglican brand.[7] Arguably the best such proposal was to employ Margaret in her various media roles. Veteran Sydney journalist and blogger John Sandeman viewed Margaret as 'the secret weapon behind Sydney Anglicans' high profile in the media.'[8] Moreover, 'most Australian Christians will complain about how the mass media deals with their church, or Christianity itself. It's rare to see someone set out to deal with this problem and even rarer to see someone succeed, not just once but many times. Margaret Rodgers, who ran media relations for the Sydney Anglicans for a decade and a half, fitted the third category exactly.'[9]

She was the reason the Sydney Diocese rose to punch above its weight in the media. In Australia's most competitive media market, the Anglicans got a lot of surprisingly positive coverage. Margaret was a master tactician at the media game: she knew the power of rarity, reserving Peter Jensen for the right sort of stories, sending out other spokespeople for day to day combat.[10]

---

6 Letter from Margaret Rodgers to Archbishop Marcus Loane, 8 Dec 1975, Sydney Diocesan Archives.

7 For example, in 1992 the Standing Committee formulated a "media plan for the 90s," a recommendation to the Council of Anglican Information Office in connection with Mr Kel Richards, referred to in minutes of Standing Committee, Anglican Diocese of Sydney, 27 Jul 1992, 111.

8 John Sandeman, 'Margaret Rodgers, Christian communicator dies,' *Eternity News*, 1 Jun 2014, https://www.eternitynews.com.au/archive/margaret-rodgers-christian-communicator-dies/#:~:text=News%20%7C%20John%20 Sandeman,their%20church%2C%20or%20Christianity%20itself..

9 Sandeman, 'Margaret Rodgers, Christian communicator dies,'.

10 Sandeman, 'Margaret Rodgers, Christian communicator dies,'.

Margaret wrote numerous articles and in later years her media advisory role for the Archbishop was the envy of other dioceses and especially the Primate's office.

Strategy and tactics

What is sometimes overlooked is the strategic role that Margaret's media comments played in public life, especially in her role as Research Officer with General Synod. Where others may have spoken in platitudes or rebuffed journalists, Margaret knew how to manage information feeds and provided first-rate copy for media organisations, even though some of her colleagues may have preferred no publicity at all.

For example, in 1987 *The Canberra Times* reported Deaconess Margaret Rodgers as calling on 'Anglican parishioners to admit they had 'failed as a church to deal with [the problem of domestic violence] adequately,'' and closed the story with another quote by Rodgers: 'Obviously any woman who has been bashed and violated by a man would find it difficult to talk to a [clergy]man.'[11]

Similarly, General Synod's Social Responsibilities Commission published a report in 1989 encouraging bishops to establish a uniform policy and practice regarding divorced Anglicans intending to remarry. Margaret is reported to have called the church's current policy on remarriage 'inconsistent' and in many cases producing 'negative results'. Demonstrating her capacity for deploying nuance and diplomacy on controversial matters, she affirmed that 'the church would always regard marriage as a lifelong commitment,' but added, quoting the report: 'The Commission contends, however, that translating theological positions into pastoral practices which have the care of people and the development of mature personal relationships as their primary aim will not erode the importance of marriage in this society ... Rather, it will demonstrate that the Anglican Church is more concerned about pastoral care than an apparent theological legalism.'[12]

Media statements often served tactical purposes. In an article in *The Sydney Morning Herald* in 1994, for example, Margaret suggested that the Anglican Church was 'on the brink of a controversy potentially

---

11 Margaret Rodgers, 'Clergy 'unhelpful' over domestic violence', *The Canberra Times*, 3 Dec 1987, 7.
12 Margaret Rodgers, 'Church to rule on remarriage', *The Canberra Times*, 9 Aug 1989, 7.

more divisive than women's ordination' – namely, lay presidency at the Lord's Supper.[13] Historian and Anglican priest Tom Frame makes much of this comment, arguing that Margaret's purpose in commenting on the policy 'was presumably to draw out its opponents.'[14] Perhaps he was right.

A theological rationale

Self-promotion was not one of Margaret's strong points: she preferred her achievements to speak for themselves. This makes it difficult to identify a particular theological basis for her media work. Yet there are occasional clues. In 2008, she wrote at length on the role of media in promoting the Christian faith. Quoting evangelical statesman John Stott, she said:

> [Stott's] call for radical discipleship and gospel proclamation is both urgent and necessary. The preaching of the gospel of God's forgiveness and saving grace for repentant sinners through Christ Jesus is the essential message that ought to be the focus and burden of every Christian preacher to the citizens of the secularized, relativist and materialist world of today.[15]

Since most people today rarely enter a gospel-saturated church, she suggested, 'they must be first touched, or have their consciences stirred, and initial interest piqued and gained through media communication avenues.'[16] She commends Archbishop Peter Jensen's strategic use of the media, especially his 2005 Boyer Lectures,[17] and adds:

> He does not present as a politician, or a specialist commentator on every issue under the sun, but as a

---

13 Margaret Rodgers, 'Now for the next Anglican controversy', *Sydney Morning Herald,* 10 May 1994, 12.

14 Tom Frame, *Anglicans in Australia* (Sydney: UNSW Press, 2007), 182; Tom Frame, 'The distinctive heritage of Australian Anglicans,' *Sewanee Theological Review* 52 (2), 2009, 154f.

15 Margaret Rodgers, 'Can you believe what you read?' in *Preach or Perish: Reaching the Hearts and Minds of the World Today*, ed. Donald Howard (Camden, NSW: privately published, 2008), 205.

16 Rodgers, 'Can you believe what you read?', 206.

17 See https://www.abc.net.au/listen/programs/bigideas/2005-boyer-lectures-by-dr-peter-jensen-lecture-one/3316646. Published as Peter Jensen, *The Future of Jesus: Does He Have a Place in Our World?* (2nd edition; Kingsford, NSW: Matthias Media, 2008).

Christian theologian and preacher who is willing to bring his Bible-informed Christian mind into public discussions of the critical issues of the day. To earn its place, Christian witness should be encased with winning persuasion and flair ... Christians should not attempt to force their views upon others; they should rather aim to convince their hearers with reasoned and informed debate. Media in all forms provide a tremendous setting to further this aim.[18]

Similarly, in her acceptance letter to Archbishop Peter Jensen on appointment as his media relations officer in October 2003, she said, 'I believe there will be many more opportunities for gospel proclamation through the media work.'[19] That was her primary purpose and aim.

Ecumenical work

When Margaret Rodgers was made a Member of the Order of Australia, the nation's highest civilian honour, in January 2014, it was for 'significant service to the Anglican Church of Australia through governance and representational roles, and to ecumenical affairs.' What were these ecumenical affairs, and why was a Sydney Anglican laywoman at the centre of them?

Ecumenical Affairs Committee

In one sense, ecumenism came to the Sydney Synod with the establishment of an Ecumenical Affairs Committee (EAC) in October 1974. Margaret was elected unopposed to this committee on 20 November 1978 (and to Standing Committee on 11 December 1978), and faithfully served for many years. Her predecessor at Deaconess House, Deaconess Mary Andrews (1915–1996), was also an active member of the EAC.[20]

The EAC's brief was massive: to 'serve, advise and inform the Diocese in regard to ecumenical matters'; to study theological and practical issues arising from such matters; to initiate and encourage discussions

18 Rodgers, 'Can you believe what you read?', 207.
19 Letter from Margaret Rodgers to Peter Jensen, 15 Oct 2003, Sydney Diocesan Archives.
20 For example, Deaconess Mary Andrews co-authored an EAC paper addressing a World Council of Churches document by Professor Klaas Runia titled, 'Theological problems concerning the W.C.C.'s Programme to Combat Racism' (1975).

within the Diocese and with other denominations on relevant matters; to monitor the development of 'church union schemes' in Australia; and to inform the Diocese concerning the programs of a wide range of ecumenical conciliar bodies including the World Council of Churches, the Christian Conference of Asia, the Australian Council of Churches and its NSW State Council (the NSW Ecumenical Council), the (evangelical) NSW Council of Churches, the Evangelical Alliance, and the NSW Inter-Church Trade and Industry Commission. By 1989, the exhausted and depleted committee had effectively ceased to function. In a memo to the Diocesan Secretary in March 1989, Bishop Donald Cameron advised that 'there is limited interest in institutional ecumenism in the Diocese of Sydney.'[21]

Ecumenical Working Group

In 1990, the EAC was disbanded and Synod established a new *ad hoc* Ecumenical Working Group (EWG) whose first major task was to analyse preliminary documents relating to the World Council of Churches Assembly to be held in Canberra in 1991 and report to the Synod Standing Committee with a view to informing the Diocese generally on the issues at stake. Key EWG players were Bishop P R Watson, Rev R H Avery, and Deaconess Margaret Rodgers.[22]

NSW Council of Churches

There was much ecumenical work beyond the Diocese. For many years, for example, Margaret served as an Anglican representative on the executive of the NSW Council of Churches, and as a director of NSW Council of Churches Broadcasters Pty Ltd, which managed the Council's Sunday broadcasting on Sydney radio station 2CH. From 2008–2010, she served as the first woman president of the NSW Council of Churches.[23]

---

21 Memo from Donald Cameron to Diocesan Secretary, 9 Mar 1989, held by Sydney Diocesan Archives. On Don Cameron's considered views regarding ecumenism, see his paper titled, 'Ecumenism as I see it,' August 1986, in Ewan Donald Cameron Correspondence 1974–1990, Ecumenical Affairs Committee Minutes [1993/057/052].
22 Minutes of Standing Committee, 29 Oct 1990; 17 Dec 1990; 25 Feb 1991, Sydney Diocesan Archives.
23 NSW Council of Churches, 'NSW Council of Churches elects first woman president,' media release, 3 July 2008.

I observed Margaret at work in executive meetings of the NSW Council of Churches for several years. She was not the sole woman Council member; other long-term members included Mrs Leslie Hicks. Unlike many of her male colleagues, Margaret spoke only when she had something substantive or new to contribute to discussions, and she did not suffer fools gladly. The Rev Dr Ross Clifford and I used to travel together to Council meetings, and on the way back to Morling College after my first meeting he said to me, 'Margaret's good value. Don't be surprised if she appears to ignore you. When she needs your help, she will let you know.' He was right: the time came when she sought me out, and for my part I found her helpful, thoughtful, kind and reliable.

Before my time, Margaret worked closely with the Rev Bernard Judd (1918–1999), who presented weekly broadcasts on 2CH for 27 years. When he retired from this role in 1996, the Council appointed Dr Clifford for a short time, then invited Margaret to be writer and presenter, a service she continued to provide for 13 years. At the time, I served as the Council's Public Affairs Director, writing research reports and lobbying state and federal politicians on issues of interest to the Council of Churches. In July 2009, Margaret announced to the board that she would step down from her radio work and that I would succeed her.[24]

This came as a surprise to me. I said to her, 'What's the brief?' She replied, 'I asked Bernard Judd that question, and he said, "Christian social commentary"'. So it was that I came to write and present the Council's 'Sunday editorials' on 2CH for more than six years before passing the baton to Russell Powell in January 2016.

Another story from the NSW Council of Churches illustrates Margaret's attention to detail and singular passion for promoting the gospel of Christ. In 2006, along with many other agencies, the Council contributed a formal statement to an independent publication calling on Australian faith communities to take principled action to combat climate change. At a subsequent Council executive meeting, interest was expressed in 'endorsing' the document. Margaret intervened, insisting that we merely 'acknowledge' it. When challenged, she replied, 'If you had read all the statements, you would have observed that the Hindu statement refers to "Lord Shri Krishna," and there is only one Lord, the

24 Minutes of a board meeting of NSW Council of Churches Broadcasters Pty Ltd, 21 July 2009, author's personal files.

Lord Jesus Christ. We cannot in good conscience "endorse" a statement recognising the authority of the "Lord" Krishna.'[25]

General Synod

On the national front, Margaret was a member of the Standing Committee of the General Synod of the Anglican Church in Australia from 1981–2000. She served as Research Officer for the General Synod Office from 1985–1993, based at St Andrew's House, Sydney, where she engaged with a wide range of issues in theology, policy and practice. She worked with all the commissions of General Synod, with special attention given to the Doctrine Commission, the Missionary and Ecumenical Commission, the Social Responsibilities Commission, and the Task Force on Mission, Evangelism, Ministry and Training.[26]

Margaret's research work with General Synod – information-gathering, analysis, evaluation, synthesis, report writing, networking, representation, and publicity – deserves separate academic attention. Here I will briefly mention a few of the highlights of which I am aware. In 1989, there was a large report co-authored by Michael Horsburgh and Margaret Rodgers on remarriage in the Anglican Church.[27]

In 1990, she wrote a report titled, 'The future life and direction of the Australian Council of Churches: A Response from the Anglican Church of Australia,' in which she observed that Anglicans strongly supported actions that would 'facilitate cooperation and understanding between the churches, and would initiate common action on prophetic, human rights and justice issues. Indeed, it might almost be said that Anglicans expect the ACC to act as their ecumenical conscience.'[28] Yet, in her conclusion she warned that such support 'also obviates the need

---

25 *Common Belief: Australia's Faith Communities on Climate Change* (Sydney: The Climate Institute, 2006), https://d3n8a8pro7vhmx.cloudfront.net/arrcc/pages/61/attachments/original/1443343972/Common_Belief.pdf?1443343972, (accessed 26 March 2024). For the Hindu statement see page 24.
26 Michael Horsburgh & Margaret Rodgers, *In Penitence and Hope: Remarriage and the Anglican Church of Australia. General Synod Paper No. 1* (Sydney: Anglican General Synod Social Responsibilities Commission, 1989), 1.
27 Horsburgh & Rodgers, *In Penitence and Hope.*
28 Report dated 22 June 1990, in Ewan Donald Cameron Correspondence 1974–1990, Ecumenical Affairs Committee Minutes [1993/055], Sydney Diocesan Archives.

for the [Anglican] Church itself to initiate and engage in ecumenism apart from membership of the Australian Council of Churches.'

In 1992 there was a book-length publication, co-edited with the Right Rev Maxwell Thomas, Chairman of the Doctrine Commission, on a theology of the human person.[29] Also in 1992, Margaret authored a report to the Bishops' Conference which collated responses from the Diocesan bishops on ecclesiastical record-keeping practices relating to baptism, admissions to communion, confirmation, trends in adult baptism and confirmation, and related issues. Margaret offered two pages of recommendations for reform.[30] In 1994, Margaret co-authored a report on Anglican clergy marriage breakdown, drawing on findings of a survey she designed based on a similar survey conducted by Roger Hennessey in the United Kingdom.[31]

In her role as Research Officer for General Synod, Margaret was also a delegate to general meetings of the Australian Council of Churches. When the ACC was restructured to create the National Council of Churches in Australia, she was appointed as a member of the NCCA executive from 1994-1997.

Anglican Consultative Council

There was also participation in meetings of the Anglican Consultative Council, a gathering of the global Anglican Communion. Margaret attended ACC meetings in Wales (1990), Panama (1996), Dundee (1999), and Hong Kong (2002), and attended the Lambeth Conference of Anglican Bishops as a media officer in 1998. Reports of all these meetings were circulated.

In 1996, Archbishop Harry Goodhew wrote to Mr Warwick Olson, chairman of the Anglican Media Council, supporting the notion that the Diocese had 'a role to play beyond its own borders.' He argued that 'it is all too easy for the antipodes to be forgotten in the world church,

---

29 Margaret Rodgers & Maxwell Thomas (eds), *A Theology of the Human Person* (North Blackburn, Vic.: Collins Dove, 1992). The Appendix reproduced General Synod Paper No. 3 on 'A Christian discussion of sexuality.'

30 Margaret Rodgers, *Report to the Bishops' Conference: Survey on Baptism, Admission to Holy Communion, Confirmation* (Sydney: Anglican Synod Office, 1992).

31 April Hyde, Margaret Rodgers & Michael Horsburgh, *A Godly Model: A Study of Clergy Marriage Breakdown in the Anglican Church of Australia* (Sydney: Anglican General Synod Social Responsibilities Commission, 1994).

particularly in the Anglican Communion. Margaret Rodgers' presence, along with that of Robert Tong as a delegate, will, in my judgment, help us to be seen and known.'[32]

Christian Conference of Asia

Margaret also participated as an Anglican delegate to the Christian Conference of Asia (CCA), a regional ecumenical organisation and forum for Christian unity and cooperation. She was elected to the CCA General Committee in June 1990 and served as CCA President from 1995–2000. As well as analysing and circulating various CCA reports, Margaret wrote detailed accounts of CCA proceedings and her personal experiences and observations for the benefit of General Synod and the Australian Council of Churches.[33]

World Council of Churches

In 1980, Margaret was an Anglican observer at the WCC Commission on World Mission and Evangelism conference in Melbourne. She was also involved in subsequent WCC meetings, notably the 1991 Seventh Assembly in Canberra, where she was an original signatory to a critical 'Letter to Churches and Christians worldwide from participants who share evangelical perspectives.'[34]

Rationale for ecumenical engagement

What can we say about Margaret Rodgers' approach to ecumenical engagement? Her commitment and perseverance are evident. As I said earlier, Margaret rarely spoke about herself. There is one place, however, where she outlined a considered personal rationale for engagement in ecumenical affairs. At a conference in Canterbury, UK, in 1993, Margaret was invited to formally respond to a paper by Bishop Michael Nazir Ali on 'Scripture in ecumenical dialogue.' Her response was published, and in it she makes two remarkable disclosures. First,

---

32 Letter from Archbishop Harry Goodhew to Warwick Olson, 3 May 1996, Sydney Diocesan Archives.

33 For example, 'Report of a visit of a delegation from the Christian Conference of Asia to the Churches in China, November 1988' (14pp); and 'Report to the Australian Council of Churches: Christian Conference of Asia Assembly' (6pp), held in Manila, Philippines. Both reports held by Sydney Diocesan Archives.

34 'Evangelical perspectives from Canberra,' *Transformation*, July/September 1991, 18–20.

Margaret describes a local ecumenical gathering between parishioners from her local Anglican Church in Newtown, Sydney, and the local Catholic parish to discuss the Anglican-Roman Catholic International Commission (ARCIC) text, *Salvation and the Church*. She writes:

> A good deal of work had been done by a group appointed by the two Archbishops to prepare studies on this ARCIC text. When our people from St Stephen's met with the people from St Joseph's the discussions were about everything else but the said text. People told each other their faith stories, they were so excited to be together. For they saw the value in their meeting and said they did not want to talk about *Salvation and the Church*. It belonged to the theologians, not to them. If we are addressing the issues of ecumenical dialogue we need to take this into account. I fear our multi-lateral and bi-lateral conversations would appear to be of only peripheral interest to most people in the pews![35]

Second, Margaret observed that:

> When I engage in ecumenical discussion, like everyone else, I take my own presuppositions and assumptions with me. I have been formed in an evangelical Anglican context which gives priority to the Scriptures as the sole rule and standard [of faith and life] and which regards the Scripture specialist as the most essential contributor to theological discussion. Our theological and social/ethical work always commences with a careful review of the relevant Scriptural teaching and we move from the Scriptural perspective we thereby deduce into the issue which is our focus. We move from Scripture to context, and hopefully we bring a Scripturally informed mind and conscience to the issue. There is a danger to this, of course. It is that one can spend so much time on an investigation into the real meaning of the text in the context of the time in which it was written that the whole endeavour is focused on that question, and the process can descend into irrelevancy in regard to our

35 Margaret Rodgers, 'Scripture in ecumenical dialogue: A response to Bishop Michael Nazir Ali,' in *The Anglican Communion and Scripture: Papers from the First International Consultation of the Evangelical Fellowship in the Anglican Communion, Canterbury, UK, June 1993*, ed. John Stott (Carlisle, UK: EFAC/Regnum Books, 1996), 97.

own contemporary questions... I am always grateful for the rich diversity of people and life situations which I meet in ecumenical circles and I benefit greatly from the insight I am given into the reality of the life of many people in our world. I hear the cry for justice and my heart echoes it, but I still wish to move from Scripture to context. I do not regard this approach as an example of the imperialism of Western Scriptural method but rather as a model of Scriptural inquiry appropriate to every culture which allows one to bring the word of the Gospel to bear upon culture and context – a priority of Scripture and Gospel over culture and context – including my own.[36]

Conclusion

The work of Deaconess Margaret Rodgers in the public sphere and beyond the Diocese of Sydney was astonishing for its intentionality, its professionalism, its notable intellectual calibre, its demonstration of theological skill and diplomacy, its warm evangelical spirituality, its diversity, and its longevity. Sydney Anglican Archbishop Glenn Davies summed up Rodgers' contribution to church life, describing her as 'for many years the leading laywoman of the Diocese of Sydney,' and 'a warrior for Christ, not ashamed of the gospel and not afraid to confront those with whom she disagreed, but always with a winsome smile and a heartfelt desire to see Christ honoured in all areas of her life.' [37] As John Sandeman eloquently put it, her power and influence 'puzzled everyone, except for those who worked with her and knew that talent had risen to the top.'[38]

---

36 Rodgers, "Scripture in ecumenical dialogue," 103. She continues: 'The more prevalent hermeneutical method within WCC discussions gives priority to context and one moves from that into the Scripture. The danger of this approach is that the Scriptural work becomes irrelevant or else the Word is read only through the lens of the context. The meaning of the text in its original context becomes a word from the past, a mere historical irrelevancy. This hermeneutical approach has developed in recent years in that WCC stream of activity called Church and Society, which is the home of many we might feel tempted to call "fundamentalist liberals".' (103f).

37 Benson, 'Margaret Amelia Rodgers', ADEB.

38 Sandeman, 'Margaret Rodgers, Christian communicator dies,' Eternity News, 1 Jun 2014.

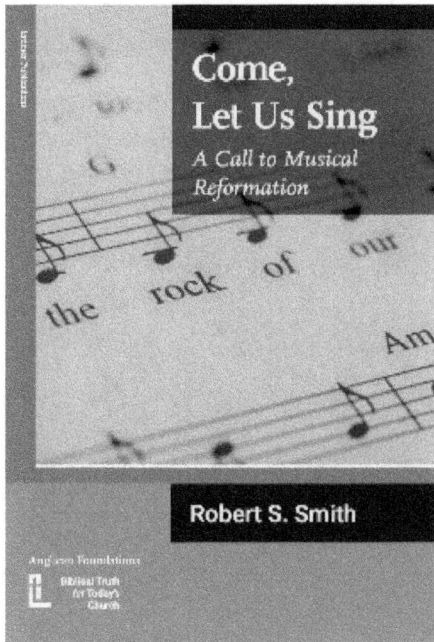

Come, Let Us Sing seeks to help us reform the musical dimension of church life by bringing biblical clarity to two key questions: Why do we come together? and Why do we sing together?

In answer to the first, Robert Smith navigates a path through the contemporary 'worship word wars', concluding that we gather both to worship God and to encourage others. Two questions must, therefore, be asked of everything we do: Does it glorify God? and Does it edify others?

As to why we sing, Smith unpacks three principal functions of congregational singing in Scripture – as a way of praising, a way of praying and a way of preaching. In so doing, he explores the necessity of singing scriptural truth, the value of psalmody, the place of emotions, the role of our bodies, and how singing expresses and enriches our unity.

Come, Let Us Sing is a timely call for the church to reclaim its biblical musical heritage and reform its musical practice.

Other recommendations

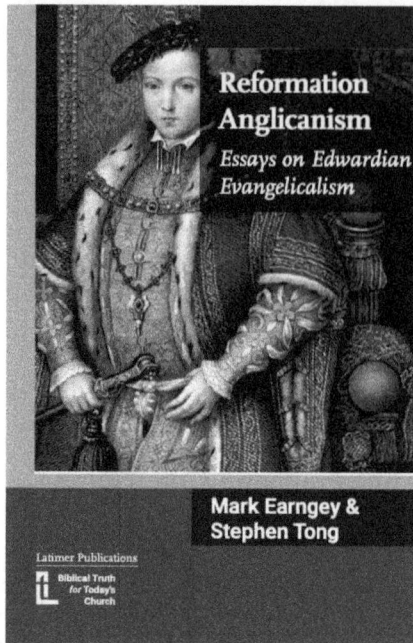

Reformation Anglicanism: Essays on Edwardian Evangelicalism is a superb set of essays arising from the Moore Theological College symposium on Reformation Anglicanism held in 2019. Featuring essays from various reformation scholars, this collection of articles focuses on some foundational documents (e.g. *Book of Homilies, Articles of Religion*) and foundational reformers (e.g. Thomas Cranmer, Martin Bucer, Heinrich Bullinger) involved with the English Reformation, and its Edwardian phase in particular. This edited volume not only offers a sustained focus on the often-neglected mid-Tudor phase of the Reformation but explores new avenues of research on overlooked subjects such as the *45 Articles* the *Reformatio Legum Ecclesiasticarum*, the ministry of John Hooper, and the memory of Martin Bucer. Students and scholars alike will benefit from this fresh examination of these anchors of Anglicanism which were hotly contested both then, and now.

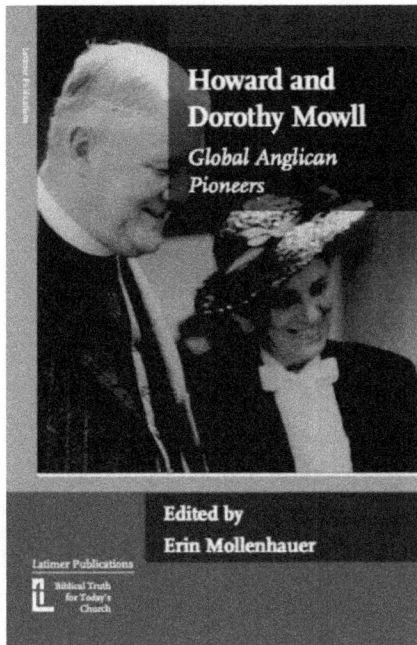

Howard and Dorothy Mowll

Global Anglican Pioneers

Edited by
Erin Mollenhauer

Latimer Publications

Biblical Truth for Today's Church

Howard Mowll was the enterprising and indefatigable Archbishop of Sydney from 1934 to 1958. At once robustly Anglican and evangelical in outlook and policy, he set the diocese of Sydney on the course it has followed to the present day.

Originating in the Moore College Library Day of 2021, the essays in this book cover previously overlooked and neglected aspects of Mowll's leadership and administration as well as providing new insights into and fresh perspectives on his life and work in Sydney.

They also give due attention to the equally remarkable contribution of Mowll's wife, Dorothy. Based on extensive archival research, and paying attention to the context of mid-twentieth century Australia, these essays begin the task of historical assessment by both extending and qualifying the biography provided by Marcus Loane in the immediate aftermath of Mowll's death. Was Mowll one of the two truly great Bishops/Archbishops of Sydney, as Peter Jensen suggests in the Introduction? This book both invites and enables readers to decide for themselves.

www.ingramcontent.com/pod-product-compliance
Lightning Source LLC
Chambersburg PA
CBHW021146020426
42331CB00005B/923